W9-BBR-504

A *Gardener's* LATIN

A *Country Living Gardener* Book

A
Gardener's
LATIN

Richard Bird

Illustrated by Cathy Morley

HEARST BOOKS
NEW YORK

Copyright © by 1999 Hearst Communications, Inc., and Salamander Books Ltd.

All rights reserved. No part of this book may be reproduced or utilized in any
form or by any means, electronic or mechanical, including photocopying,
recording, or by any information storage or retrieval system, without permission
in writing from the Publisher. Inquiries should be addressed to Permissions
Department, William Morrow and Company Inc., 1350 Avenue of the Americas,
New York, N.Y. 10019.

It is the policy of William Morrow and Company, Inc., and its imprints and
affiliates, recognizing the importance of preserving what has been written, to
print the books we publish on acid-free paper, and we exert our best efforts
to that end.

Library of Congress Cataloging-in-Publication Data

Country Living Gardener A Gardener's Latin.

p.cm.
Includes bibliographical references (p.) and index.
ISBN 0-688-16779-9
1. Botany--Terminology.   2. Latin language, Medieval and modern--Glossaries,
vocabularies, etc. 3. English language--Glossaries, vocabularies, etc.
I. Country living gardener. II. Title: A Gardener's Latin
QK10.C68   1999
580'. 1'4--dc21   98-43254
                                                                   CIP

Printed in the United Arab Emirates

First Edition

1 2 3 4 5 6 7 8 9 10

www. williammorrow.com

CONTENTS

INTRODUCTION

The need for a universal language for plants is twofold. First, a plant should be represented by a single name wherever that plant is talked or written about. The name should be the same in Russia as it is in the United States. A different name in each inevitably leads to confusion: a bluebell in England is a different plant from that known as a bluebell in Scotland, for example.

Looking at it another way, the plant known throughout the world as *Lotus corniculatus* has over 70 different local names in Britain alone. When the modern system of naming was devised by Linnaeus in 1753, Latin was still the language of science, as well as being the only universal language, so it was the obvious choice for the names.

However, although botanical naming is always thought of as Latin, it does contain words derived from many other languages, in particular Greek. Nearly twenty years before he set about naming plants, Linnaeus had devised a system of classification into which he fitted all plants so that their relationships were clear. Thus he brought together all the buttercups into a group that he named *Ranunculus*. This group he called a genus (plural genera) and the individual plants that made up the genus were known as species. He also brought together all the groups or genera that were related into a larger group which he called a family. Thus *Caltha* (marsh marigold), *Anemone*, and *Clematis* are botanically closely related to *Ranunculus* and so they are put into one family. The family name is based on the most typical genus of that family and so in this case it is known as Ranunculaceae.

Although the family is an important part of the classification of plants it does not appear in the name. The first element is the genus. The names given to different genera are derived from different sources. In some cases they are descriptive, in others they are the name by which they have been known since ancient times. Some names are even made-up ones. Many of these names are well known to gardeners, for example *Hosta*, *Fuchsia*, *Chrysanthemum*, and *Delphinium*.

The second part of the name is the species and refers to individual plants rather than a group of them. This name is often descriptive in some way of the plant. Thus *Geranium pyrenaicum* is the geranium from the Pyrenées, while *Geranium tuberosum* has tubers. If several members of the same genus are mentioned, then the second and subsequent mentions usually have the name of the genus represented by an initial. Thus *Geranium tuberosum* could here be represented as *G. tuberosum*.

Since the names are often based on Latin, the gender of the species must agree with that of the genus. This is most easily shown in genera ending in -us (masculine), -a (feminine) and -um (neuter).

Thus one sees *Hosta gracillima* and *Geranium nodosum*. If the specific name is derived from another language, then it takes on the appropriate ending in that language.

Botanists often need to break species down into subspecies and will often add a third element to the name, sometimes using the abbreviation ssp,

but not always. Thus *Geranium sessiliflorum* ssp. *novae-zelandiae* may be listed without the ssp. If the plant is not important enough to be called a subspecies, then botanists use the term variety, abbreviated to var. *Geranium sanguineum* var. *striatum* is an example.

Horticulture also provides another element, namely the cultivar. This is a form of the plant that is worth distinguishing for horticultural purposes, but is not worth differentiating botanically because a cultivar only varies by some superficial aspect, such as color, from the typical species. Cultivars are shown in single quotation marks – *Geranium sylvaticum* 'Mayflower', for example. Cultivar names should not be in Latin, although some names still exist from the time before the rule forbidding them came into existence.

One further thing remains to be explained. Names sometimes include an x. This indicates that the plant is a hybrid, *Geranium* x *oxonianum,* for example. If both parents are known they are often given in the name; for example *Passiflora* x *caeruleoracemosa* is a cross between *Passiflora caerulea* and *Passiflora racemosa*.

PREFIXES

Most specific names are composed of simple words, such as the word *alba* meaning white, but there is also an important group of compound words, made up from two words. Thus the specific name *argophyllum* is made up of two elements: *argo*, white, and *phyllum*, leaf, i.e., white-leaved (*Olearia argophylla*, the white-leaved olearia, for example). Many words are constructed in this way. Numbers of various parts of the plant are quite common – *triphyllum*, three-leaved, or *hexandra*, six-stamened, for example.

Most prefixes are either adjectives or adverbs showing size or position. Examples of size can be seen in *macro-*, large (*Aster macrophyllus,* the large-leaved aster); *parvi-*, small (*Cyclamen parviflorum*, the small-flowered cyclamen). Other attributes may be used, such as *atro-*, meaning dark (as in *atrosanguineus*, dark blood-red). Position is also frequently seen; *transcaucasicus* means just that, "transcaucasian" – from right across the Caucasian mountains. Sometimes the prefix is another plant; *salicifolia* means willow-leaved, from *salix*, willow, and *folia*, leaved.

Unfortunately some prefixes have a wide range of meanings. *Sub*, for example, means not only the position below, but also nearly, somewhat, or not quite. Thus *subalpinus* means below alpine levels, but *subcaeruleus* means slightly blue or bluish, while *subcordatus* can be interpreted as rather heart-shaped. On the whole, though, most prefixes are quite clear in their meaning. Build up a store of prefixes and suffixes (see pages 12–13) that are common to many words and you will have the building blocks of a considerable vocabulary.

Cosmos atrosanguineus

Dianthus superbus

Phlox subulata

actino-	radiating
aniso-	unequal, uneven
ante-	before
argo-	white
atro-	dark
bi-, bis-	twice, two
calli-, calo-	beautiful
chlori-	separate
de-	downward
fici-	fig-like
heli-	sun
hex-	six
hyper-	above
hypo-	below
macro-	large, long
magnus-	large
neo-	new
non-	not, un-
parvi-	small
poly-	many
post-	behind, post
pre-	before, in front of
pro-	before, in front of
ptero-	winged
quadri-	four
re-	back
salici-	willow-like
sub-	below, partially, somewhat, nearly
super-	above
trans-	through, across
tri-	three
uni-	one
xero-	dry
xylo-	woody

SUFFIXES

Suffixes have an affinity with prefixes, as they are also combined with other words, but this time they are added to the end. They might not be quite so easy to identify, but as you become familiar with more botanical names, so the suffixes will become self-evident, if only because they crop up frequently. Sometimes suffixes are combined simply with prefixes – *macrorrhizus* (*macro-*, large or long, *-rrhizus,* rooted). In other cases a suffix is attached to a noun, as in the combination of *rupes* (rocks) with *-estris* (place of growth) to form *rupestris* (growing in rocky places). Some of the most frequently occurring nouns are places to which *-ensis* is attached – *stevenagensis*, from Stevenage, for example. Possibly the most frequently met suffixes are those denoting the major parts of the plant – the flower, the stem, or the leaves – which are prefaced by some qualifier. Thus, *phyllus* is leaved, so *triphyllus* may well be used to describe a plant that is three-leaved, while a plant with many leaves may carry the species name *polyphyllus*. One named *macropetala* is likely to have large or long petals. Another suffix, *-folius*, also refers to the leaves or foliage – *rubrifolius*, red-leaved, is one example; *-florus* means flowered and is often used with a variety of prefixes to form words such as *densiflorus,* meaning dense-flowered, or *parviflorus*, small-flowered.

Some endings add a dimunitive quality to the description. Thus *ruber* is red but *rubellus* is reddish. At the other extreme is the superlative *-issimus* denoting very – *spinosissimus*, very spiny, for example.

Lathyrus sylvestris

Wisteria floribunda

-*aceus* resembling
-*anthemus* flowered
-*anthus* flowered
-*ascens* becoming
-*bundus* capacity for
-*cellus* diminutive
-*color* colored
-*doxa* glory of
-*ellus* diminutive
-*ensis* country or place of origin
-*escens* becoming
-*estris* place of growth
-*fer* bearing
-*fid* divided, cleft
-*florus* flowered
-*folius* leaved
-*formis* shaped
-*icola* of, from
-*ineus, -inus* -like
-*iscus* lesser
-*issimus* very
-*nervis, -neuris* nerved, veined
-*odes, -oides* resembling, similar to
-*osma* fragrant
-*osus* abundant, plenty, large
-*partitus* parted, deeply divided
-*phorus* carrying, bearing
-*phyllus* leaved
-*quetrus* angled
-*rrhizus* rooted
-*stemon* stamened
-*stylus* styled
-*thamnus* shrub-like
-*usculus* diminutive

GENERAL PERSONALITY

Plants can be said to have a personality – a certain air about them – and this is often reflected in their names. The term *vulgare* often refers to what was considered the most common plant in the genus at the time of the naming; thus the primrose was named *Primula vulgaris*. The most common plant in any genus is, of course, going to vary depending on where you are. Just as common is a relative term, so beauty is in the eye of the beholder and plants considered attractive by some are not necessarily found to be so by others. Nevertheless, many species' names describe the beauty of a plant. The specific name *bellus* means beautiful and is fairly easy to identify; *callistus*, which means very beautiful, and *agetus*, wonderful, are less obvious. *Elegantissima* presents no surprises as it means very elegant, while *dius* shows even greater beauty since it describes a plant as belonging to the gods. *Mirabilis* also shows marked admiration for a plant as it means extraordinary, wonderful, or remarkable. *Mirandus* has the same meaning. However, there is a darker side to many plants. *Decipiens* means deceptive, while *fallax* has a false air about it. *Debilis*, as in *Sedum debilis*, is weak, feeble, or debilitated. Weak or poor plants may also be described as *inops*. As to morals, well even plants can sink low – *adulterinus* means adulterous (in other words, it hybridizes easily), while *impudicus* shows a lewd or shameless quality! Give a wide berth to anything named *infestus* as it may do just that – infest or become troublesome.

Larix decidua

Foeniculum vulgare

adulterinus adulterous, i.e.
   hybridizes easily
agetus wonderful
bellus beautiful
callistus very beautiful
communis growing in company
debilis weak, feeble
deciduus deciduous
decipiens deceptive
elegantissima very elegant
fallax false
fecundus fruitful
feris wild
floribundus free-flowering
generalis usual, prevailing, normal
illustris illustrious, brilliant
impudicus lewd, shameless
infestus dangerous, likely to
   infest, troublesome
insignis significant, striking,
   remarkable
major major, bigger, larger
mirabilis extraordinary, wonderful,
   remarkable
mirandus extraordinary, wonderful,
   remarkable
mixtus mixed
modestus modest
monstrosus abnormal, monstrous
permixtus confusing
robustus strong, growing
simplex simple
singularis singular, distinct, unusual
tristis dull, sad appearance
vulgare common

COLOR

Black and White

A garden or border of black and white flowers would cause a sensation, but, alas, there are not enough black plants to make this a practical project. Nevertheless there are plenty of plants that contain black in their name. This often refers to parts other than flowers, especially the leaves and seed. In *Helleborus niger* it is the root that is black – the flower is white! As with all colors there are grades, from black, *niger*, to *nigricans*, blackish, taking in coal black, *anthracinus*, and sooty, *fulginosus*, on the way.

Between black and white, there is, of course, gray. While there are few gray flowers, it is a popular color in the garden for foliage, especially when it is upgraded to silver. Again there are all kinds of variation on the theme. *Cinereus* is ash-gray, while plants that have a habit of turning ash-gray are sometimes known as *cinerascens*. *Griseus* is that pearly gray that can be seen on the hairy undersides of the leaves of *Ceanothus griseus*, while *incanus* is a more hoary gray. Silver hairs on the leaves are responsible for many of these names, including, as often as not, the term *argenteus*, silver or silvery.

White is a very popular color for flowers and it is well represented in their naming. The most common, *alba*, white, is one of the first specific names that many gardeners ever learn. *Albescens* also means white, but with the sense of turning white, perhaps from yellow or pink. *Lacteus* has a small touch of yellow in it – a milky white. For that glistening snow white, *niveus* is the name to look out for, and *zaleucum*, as in *Rhododendron zaleucum*, has a similar meaning.

Centaurea nigra

Nymphaea alba

alba white
albescens turning white
albicans becoming white, off-white
albidus whitish
albomaculatus white-spotted
albopictus painted white
albovariegatus white variegations
anthracinus coal-black
argenteus silver, silvery
argo- white
cinerascens becoming ash gray
cinereus ash gray
dealbatus whitened
fulgineus sooty
fulginosus sooty
griseus gray, pearly gray
incanus hoary gray
lactescens becoming milky white
lacteus milky white
lividus lead color, gray
margaritus pearly
niger black
nigrescens black
nigricans blackish
nigropunctatus spotted black
nivalis snow white
niveus snow white
nivosus snow white
plumbeus lead gray
pullus raven black, pitch black
ravus grayish
subcanus slightly gray
vestalis white
virginalis virginal white
zaleucus very white

COLOR

Red and Pink

One of the first things that many people notice about a plant is the color of its flower and, to a lesser extent, the color of the leaves. Color, therefore, plays an important part when it comes to naming plants.

The reds are among the most striking, but there is no one shade. They vary from the blood reds to the flame reds tinged with orange, and to those reds tinged with purple. All these variations are reflected in the names.

As with so many botanical names, the meaning often becomes quite obvious if you think of a similar word in English. Plain, simple red is *ruber*, easy to remember if you think of ruby. Scarlet is *coccineus*, which is related to the word cochineal. Blood red has a sanguine look to it, hence the name *sanguineus*, as in the well-known *Geranium sanguineum*, the bloody cranesbill.

Flammeus and *igneus* both describe flaming or "ignited" red.

Many others are not quite so obvious and need to be learned. For example, some plants start one color and change to red; *rubescens* or *erubescens* in the name describes this phenomenon.

While the reds are often hot and exciting, the pinks are softer and more romantic. As with all colors the various shades are reflected in different names. For example, rosy pink, or rose, is often given in plant names as *roseus*. Equally familiar, flesh pink is referred to in terms related to the word carnal, namely *carneus* or *incarnatus*. Coral pink is referred to as *coralloides* or *corallinus*.

Aesculus carnea

Centranthus ruber

carneus flesh-colored
cinnabarinus vermilion, cinnabar-red
coccineus scarlet
corallinus coral pink
coralloides coral pink
erubescens turning red
ferrugineus rust red
flammeus flame red
igneus flame red
incarnatus flesh pink
latericius brick red
miniatus cinnabar or red-lead red
porphyreus warm red
puniceus carmine red, purple-red
roseus rosy pink
rubellus reddish
rubens red
ruber red
rubescens turning red
rubicundus rubicund, ruddy
rubiginosus rusty-red
rufescens turning red
rufinus red
rufus reddish brown
russatus russet red
rutilans bright red
sanguineus blood red, sanguine
scarlatinus scarlet, bright red
vinaceus wine red
vinicolor wine red
vinosus wine red

COLOR

Blue, Violet, and Purple

Blues are becoming increasingly popular in the garden, especially in contrasting groups with yellow. They are also used with violets and purples in some more romantic settings, where they are mixed with pastel colors.

There are perhaps not as many Latin words for expressing blue, violet, and purple as there are for most of the other colors. However, there are more than enough to express the range of colors involved.

As with the Latin names for most colors, the most frequently used are quite readily understandable to the gardener; *purpurea* is purple, *lilacina* is lilac, *violaceus* is violet, and *azureus* is azure. On the blue side *caeruleus* (caerulean blue) is possibly the most commonly seen, although it is often spelled *coeruleus*. *Allium caeruleum*, *Catananche caerulea*, and *Passiflora caerulea* are three such named plants, all with blue flowers. *Cyanus* is another common term for blue or cyan.

Tone the color down a bit and you get *lilacina* (lilac) and *caesius* (lavender or grayish blue). Add a touch of red and either *ianthus* or *violaceus* can be used to describe its violet color. Add more red and purple comes into being. *Purpureus* is a common description for both flowers and leaves; preface it with *atro-* and you have dark purple.

As always, some of the color terms are used combined with suffixes denoting the part of the plant. For example, *cyaneus*, blue, occurs as *cyananthus,* with blue flowers, *cyanocarpus*, with blue fruit, and *cyanophyllus*, with blue leaves.

Digitalis purpurea

Allium caeruleum

amaranticolor purple
amethystinus violet
atropurpureus dark purple
azureus sky blue, azure
caerulescens bluish
caeruleus blue, cerulean, dark blue
caesius lavender
coerulescens bluish
coeruleus blue
cyaneus Prussian blue
ianthus violet
lilacinus lilac
lividus grayish blue
ostruthius purplish
pavonicus peacock blue
pavonius peacock blue
puniceus purple-red
purpureus purple
subcaeruleus slightly blue
violaceus violet
violescens violetish, turning violet

COLOR

Yellow and Orange

Yellow and orange are often thought of as being fall colors, but there are, in fact, flowers of these colors throughout the year, from the daffodils of spring through the daylilies of summer to the sunflowers of fall and the winter honeysuckles in the darkest months.

There are two distinct strains of yellows: the orange-yellows, which go well with other hot colors, and the green-yellows, which are much cooler and look good combined with blues.

The wide range of these yellows is reflected in the number of names. Some names may seem familiar. Canary yellow, unsurprisingly, is *canarius* (but beware: *canariensis* indicates that the plant came from the Canary Islands), while *citrinus* means lemon or citrus yellow. Plants described as *ochreus* have an ocher quality about their flowers and *sulphureus* is sulfurous or pale yellow.

There are plenty that are not so obvious, although *croceus*, indicating saffron yellow, and *aureus*, pointing to gold, as in *Alstroemeria aurea*, are still fairly easy to decipher for those with a smattering of Latin. Among those that are perhaps not so easy are *luridus*, meaning smoky or dirty yellow, *lutescens*, pale yellow or just turning yellow, and *icterinus*, which implies a jaundiced quality.

Orange is on the hot side of yellow and *aurantiacus* is one of the specific names that is frequently met in this connection, *Mimulus aurantiacus* being an example.

Beyond orange, copper is a color that is occasionally met and is likely to be covered by the name *cupreus*.

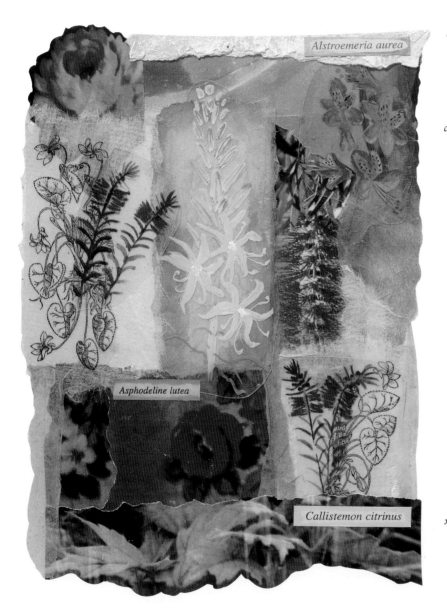

Alstroemeria aurea

Asphodeline lutea

Callistemon citrinus

aurantiacus	orange
aureus	golden
aurorius	orange
aurosus	golden
canarius	canary yellow
chryseus	golden yellow
chrysoleucus	gold and white
citrinus	lemon yellow, citrus
croceus	saffron
cupreus	coppery
flaveolus	yellowish
flavescens	turning yellow
flavus	bright yellow
fulvus	tawny, reddish yellow
galbinus	greenish yellow
giluus	dull yellow
helvolus	light yellowish brown
helvus	pale honey-colored
icterinus	yellowed, jaundiced
luridus	dirty yellow, smoky yellow
luteolus	yellowish
lutescens	pale yellow, turning yellow
luteus	yellow
ochraeus	ocher
ochroleucus	yellowish white, buff
stramineus	straw-colored
sulphureus	sulphur, pale yellow
vitellinus	egg-yolk yellow
xanthinus	yellow
xanthospilus	yellow-spotted

COLOR
Green and Brown

Green and brown are not very familiar in terms of flowers but frequently crop up in other parts of the plant. What few green flowers exist are always in vogue and anything carrying the name *viridiflorus*, green-flowered, is certain of attention.

Green, of course, often refers to the leaves. Evergreens, such as box (*Buxus*), may well have the specific name *sempervirens*, literally meaning always green. *Glaucus* is another frequently met name. This is a sea green, a green overlaid with a bluish or grayish waxy bloom, as in *Rosa glauca*. There are a whole gamut of words beginning with *vir-* which describe green in its various states; verdant is a close English word which should trigger the memory.

Browns may not seem a color with which many flowers are associated, but it is surprising how many there are, particularly when one considers how orange frequently shades into brown, as in the rudbeckias. *Ferrugineus* is rusty brown or ferruginous; *Digitalis ferruginea* and *Rhododendron ferrugineum* are two familiar plants that carry the name. In the first it is the flowers that are referred to and in the other it is the underside of the leaves. The latter example shows how important it is to look beyond the flowers when considering the names of plants. Another obvious brown is *rufus*, which is rufous or rusty brown. *Brunneus* is not too far from the word brown and should be easily recognizable. *Fuscus* is yet another word with an English equivalent, fuscous.

Digitalis ferruginea

Helleborus viridis

aeruginosus	rusty brown
aquilus	blackish brown
atrovirens	deep green
brunneus	deep brown
chlorus	yellowish green
cinnamomeus	cinnamon
euchlorus	fresh green
ferrugineus	rusty brown
flavovirens	yellowish green
fuscatus	brownish
fuscus	brown, fuscous
glaucus	glaucous green, sea green
prasinus	leek green
rufus	rufus
sempervirens	always green
spadiceus	chestnut or date brown
testaceus	brick-colored
virens	green
virescens	light green
viridescens	becoming green
viridifuscus	greenish brown
viridior	greener
viridis	green
viridissimus	very green
viridulus	greenish

MARKINGS

Although the colors and shapes of flowers, leaves, and the plant as a whole give a pretty good indication as to which plant is which, the markings on the various parts may also help to identify it. The markings are often not merely a random feature that Nature tacked onto the plant for decoration; they frequently have a function. Spots on flowers may, for example, act as guides for pollinating insects.

There is a great fascination in looking closely at flowers and enjoying the subtle variations in the way the colors have been applied – mottled, smudged, or with stripes, spots, or blotches, to name but a few. Many of these markings are reflected in the plants' names. The markings do not apply only to the flowers, but may refer to any part of the plant. Thus in *Iris reticulata* the *reticulata* refers to the netting around the corm or bulb.

However in the main it is the flowers, leaves, and sometimes the stems to which the names refer. *Variegatus*, referring to variegated leaves, must be one of the most common terms, particularly when it is used as a cultivar name, as in *Elaeagnus pungens* 'Variegata', for example. A quick glance at the leaves of *Hieraceum maculatum* will quickly show why the Latin word for "blotched" appears in the name. Similarly a look at the pure blue flowers of the common bluebell will indicate why it is *Hyacinthoides non-scriptus* or the "unmarked" hyacinthoides. Finally, it is worth avoiding the "dirty" or "sordid" flowers of *Eupatorium sordidum* if the name is anything to go by.

Calathea zebrina

Satirion maculatis

astictus unspotted, perfect
cadmicus metallic-looking
castus unspotted, pure
concolor evenly colored, uniform
conspersus scattered, speckled
decolorans discoloring, staining
diaphanus diaphanous, transparent
dichromus two-colored
digraphis lined with two colors
estriatus without stripes
fucatus painted, dyed
grammatus with raised lines
illinitus smudged
illustratus painted
inscriptus with script-like markings
iridescens iridescent
lentiginosus freckled, mottled
lepidotus scurfy, scaly
maculatus blotched, spotted
marginata edged, margined
marmoratus mottled, marbled
mediopictus striped down the middle
metallicus metallic
micans glittering
mutabilis changeable
non-scriptus unmarked
notatus spotted
occellatus eye-like
pardulinus spotted like a leopard
pallescens becoming pale
pictus painted
punctatus dotted
reticulatus netted, veined
scriptus marked with script-like
  lines
sordidus sordid, dirty-looking
variegatus variegated

SHAPE

Flower Shape

Flower shape would seem an obvious detail of a plant to use in identifying it as there seems to be an infinite variety. In many cases it is the overall shape of the flower that is considered. Bell-shaped or *campanulatus* (related to the word campanology, which means bell-ringing) is one of the most frequently encountered. It is, of course, the generic name for the bellflowers, the *Campanula*, but is also seen in such names as *Agapanthus campanulatus* or *Rhododendron campanulatum*. Similar types of names include *globularis*, round or globular, and *urceolatus*, pitcher-shaped.

One of the most common references to flower shape explains that it is double, with the name *flore-pleno*. This is also used as a cultivar or varietal name as in *Galanthus nivalis* 'Flore Pleno', the double common snowdrop.

At other times the name will refer to a distinctive feature of the flower. Flowers with lips may be referred to as *cheilanthus* (as in *Delphinium cheilanthum*) or *ringens*, two-lipped (*Salvia ringens*). Some species may be differentiated from close relatives by the fact that they are open, *chasmanthus*, or closed, *intactus*. Sometimes the descriptions of the shapes can become quite poetic. In *Cypripedium calceolus* the specific name refers to the fact that the flower is slipper-shaped, while plants with the name *tubiformis* indicate that their flowers are trumpet-shaped.

It is not only the shape of the individual flowers that are named; sometimes it is the shape of the whole flower head that is described. Thus *Campanula glomerata* has its flowers clustered together.

Enkianthus campanulatus

Aquilegia stellata

acerus without horns
aggregatus clustered together
calcaratus horned
calceolatus slipper-shaped
campanulatus bell-shaped
chasmanthus open flowers
cheilanthus lipped flowers
comosus tufts of flowers
cornutus horned
crucifer cruciform, crossed
decandrus ten-stamened
difformis misshapen
flore-pleno double-flowered
globularis ball-shaped, globular
glomeratus collected together, glomerate
hexandrus six-stamened
intactus unopened
involucratus surrounded by bracts
labiatus lip-shaped
lophanthus crested flowers
pleniflorus double flowers
plumosus feathery
racemosus in a raceme
radiosus many rayed
ringens two-lipped
sculptus sculpted, carved
scutellatus shield-shaped
sphaerocephalus round-headed
stamineus with prominent stamens
stellatus star-shaped
tubiformis trumpet-shaped
umbellatus umbelled
urceolatus pitcher-shaped

SHAPE

Leaf Shape

As we have already seen, one of the most common ways of naming a plant is to use a word that describes some aspect of it. The shape of a plant's leaves is one of the most obvious aspects to choose. Such a species name will often incorporate the suffix *folius*, *folia*, or *folium*, or alternatively *phyllus*, to indicate that it is the leaf that the name refers to and not, say, the flower. Thus, *grandifolius* refers to large leaves and *pentaphyllus* means five-leaved.

On the other hand, many specific names refer simply to a shape; *palmatum,* for example, indicates that the leaves of the plant are palmate, or like the fingers radiating from the palm of a hand.

The outline shape of the leaves is one of the first details that is noticed. Some are very distinct, such as those with round leaves, *rotundifolia*; or those that are thin and linear in shape, *linearis*. Rather than its overall shape, it may be the margins of the leaf that are its most distinctive feature and there are a number of common words that describe these. *Dentatus* indicates that the plant has a dentate or toothed margin, while one with wavy or sinuous margins might carry the specific name *sinuatus*.

The tips and base of each leaf can also be distinguishing features; *acuminatus* has a slender pointed tip, and the base of *cordatus* is cordate or heart-shaped. Not all leaves are simple, many are compound – that is, made up of a number of leaflets. *Pinnatus* means that the plant has pinnate leaves, i.e. the leaflets are arranged in pairs up the stem, for example.

Primula marginata

Achillea millefolium

alternatus alternate
bifidus bifid, deeply cleft
bifoliatus bifoliate, two leaflets
blepharophyllus fringed
caudatus tailed
chirophyllus hand-shaped
cochlearis spoon-shaped
conjunctus joined together
cordatus heart-shaped
crispus curled
dentatus toothed
depressus pressed flat downward
digitalis fingered, like digits
diphyllus two-leaved
ellipticus elliptical
emarginatus notched at the top
ensatus sword-shaped
flabellatus fan-shaped
hastatus hastate, arrow-shaped
imbricatus overlapping
incisus deeply cut
linearis narrow, linear
mucronatus mucronate, sharp tip
nervosus ribbed
nummularis round
palmatus palmate, palm-shaped
peltatus staked from the middle
petiolaris having a leaf stalk
pinnatus pinnate, leaflets on
either side of the leaf
stalk
pungens pointed
rotundatus round, rotund
sessile without stems
triplinervis three-ribbed

SHAPE

Plant Shape

Shape need not refer to just the flowers and leaves. It can, of course, also refer to the overall shape of the plant or to that of the stems.

Some words will be quite familiar. Looking at *Araucaria columnaris* it will quickly be apparent that the plant is columnar or pillar-like, while *Potentilla erecta* is erect or upright. Another familiar word is *prostratus*, prostrate, referring to a plant that grows close to the ground. *Decumbens* has the same meaning of prostrate or decumbent, although it differs slightly from *prostratus* in that it also indicates that the tips of the shoots are upright. If the shoots are creeping along the ground, the plant may be referred to as *reptans*.

Diffusus may be used to describe a plant that has a diffused shape with spreading branches, whereas a plant with the name *compactus* will be compact or dense. Plants that have their branches close together and erect are often said to be *fastigiatus* (fastigiate), while at the opposite extreme, those that are turned sharply down are *deflexus* (deflexed).

The stems are also important in naming some plants. The tree *Pinus flexilis* is so called because of its flexed or wavy stems, whereas plants with a greater tendency toward crooked stems might be given the specific name *contorta* (contorted). Another couple of relatively common names relating to plant shape are *angularis*, meaning with angular stems, and *alatus*, with winged stems. If the plant grows from a rosette, it might well be called *rosularis* and if it is without a stem, it could be known as *acaulis*.

Buddleja globosa

Nicotiana alata

Galanthus gracilis

acaulis no stem
aculeatus prickly, thorny
aculeolatus with small prickles
alatus winged
angularis angular
annulatus ringed
aphyllus without leaves
caespitosus tufted, dense clumps
capillepes slender-stalked
cappriolatus with tendrils
chamae- prostrate
cocciferus berry-bearing
columnaris columnar, pillar-like
constrictus erect, dense
contortus contorted, twisted
decumbens decumbent with upturned tips
deflexus turned sharply downward
deformis malformed, deformed
diffusus spreading
erectus erect, upright
fastigiatus with upright branches
flexuosus wavy
frutescens shrubby
furcatus forked
globosus round, globe-shaped
gracilis graceful, slender
polygyrus twining
prostratus prostrate
reptans creeping
rosularis with rosettes

TEXTURE

When designing a garden or a border it is obviously important to consider such factors as the color and shape of the plants. Another important aspect, but one that is often overlooked, is texture. Texture influences the way the light is reflected from the leaves and flowers, and can give a plant a soft velvety look or a hard, shiny appearance. Needless to say, texture is frequently reflected in plant names. On the one hand, there are words that are used to describe plants with silky or soft-textured leaves, including *bombycinus* (silky), *lanuginosus* (soft and hairy), and *ceraceus* (waxy). On the other, there are species names that describe rough textures, such as *asper* and *scaber* (rough), *coriaceus* (leathery), and *ferox*, which tells us that the plant is very prickly.

The degree of hairiness of stems and leaves is commonly reflected in names. *Adpressus* has hairs that lie flat, *ciliaris* is fringed with hairs, while *eriophorus* and *lanatus* are woolly. *Hirsutus* simply means hairy or hirsute, while *hirsutissimus* indicates that a plant is very hairy and *hispidus* that it is bristly with stiff hairs. *Pubescens* refers to plants that are downy, whereas *barbatus* means bearded. *Calvus*, on the other hand, is bald. Once the hairs get too stiff, they become thorns. *Armatus* is easy to understand as it means armed or thorny. Another word with a similar meaning is *acanthus*. Without hairs or thorns a plant may be deemed smooth or glabrous and here the specific name might be *glaber*. Not all plants are pleasant to touch, however. *Mucosus* indicates that the plant is slimy and *viscosus*, that it is viscid or sticky.

Eupatorium rugosum

Dianthus barbatus

adenophyllus	hairy leaves
adpressus	laying flat
armatus	thorny, armed
asper	rough
barbatus	bearded
bombycinus	silky
ceraceus	waxy
ciliaris	fringed with hairs
coriaceus	leathery
dealbatus	white-powdered
eriophorus	woolly
farinosus	white-powdered
ferox	very prickly
fimbriatus	fringed
fulgens	shining
glaber	smooth, glabrous
glabratus	becoming smooth
glaucus	whitish bloom
hirsutissimus	very hairy
hirsutus	hairy
hispidus	bristly, stiff hairs
laciniatus	slashed, jagged
laevigatus	smooth, polished
lanatus	woolly
lanuginosus	soft hairs
lucidus	lucid, shining
mucosus	slimy
nitidus	glossy
papyraceus	papery
pilosus	long, soft hairs
pubescens	downy
rugosus	wrinkled
scaber	rough
striatus	marked with long lines, striated
tomentosus	thickly haired
viscidus	sticky, viscid

SIZE

One very obvious characteristic of a plant is its size and, naturally, the naming of plants often reflects this. With only a small plot to furnish, the gardener might well be wise to avoid any plants with the name *gigantea* – gigantic or very large – and it may be worth double-checking on anything claiming to be *exaltus* or *excelsior*, both of which mean very large. *Ponderosus,* as its name implies, is heavy and ponderous – again, not really an attractive quality for a plant. It might be possible to get by with *magnificus* (magnificent or great) or *majesticus* (majestic), but in any case, it is worth remembering that all size is relative and what may be described as large might only be so in relation to other plants in the group. Thus *maximus*, although it means the largest, could easily be quite small.

Moving down the scale, *medium* hardly needs explanation. Then we come down in size to plants that will fit into any garden. *Minor* implies that the plant is small or at least the smaller form of something, *nanus* means dwarf, and *pygmaeus*, not surprisingly, means pigmy. The smallest plant of the genus may carry the name *minutissimus*.

Some names imply a little more than mere size. While *grandis* means large, it also has an element of grand or showy about it. *Tenuis* is thin or slender but has a touch of elegance about it. Other qualities are perhaps not so welcome; *obesus* means fat, or succulent, and *macer* is meagre, while *macellus* is only slightly less so.

Aethionema grandiflorum

Betula nana

elatus	tall
exaltus	very tall
excelsior	very tall
giganteus	gigantic
grandiflorus	large-flowered
grandifolius	large-leaved
grandis	showy, large, big
humilis	low-growing
macellus	rather meager
macer	meager
macilentus	thin
magnificus	magnificent
magnus	large, great
majesticus	majestic
maximus	largest
medius	medium, middle-sized
minimus	smallest
minor	small
minutissimus	very small, minute
minutus	small
nanus	dwarf
nanellus	very dwarf
obesus	fat, succulent
parvus	small
parvulus	very small
perpusillus	very small
ponderosus	heavy, large
praealtus	very tall
procerus	very tall
profusus	profuse, very abundant
pumilus	dwarf, small
pusillus	very small
pygmaeus	dwarf, pigmy
tenuis	thin, slender

DIRECTION

The overall appearance or character of a plant is shaped by the way the branches or stems grow. A plant with upright stems, *erectus* or *rectus*, has quite a different feel to one that is weeping or pendulous, *pendulus*. Such factors could be very important to the gardener when choosing a plant. In some cases it may be the habit of the whole plant that influences its name, but in others it may be that only a part of the plant is involved, as in *Trillium cernuum*, where it is the flower heads that are drooping, *cernuum*.

Many of the terms used to describe direction are similar to English words, which makes learning the names of plants that use them very easy. Simply remember the outstanding characteristic of the plant and you should be there. There are generally three directions to consider. Upward is an obvious direction for a plant to grow. *Verticalis*, as you would expect, means vertical or upward, while *ascendens*, ascending, is another name with a meaning that is straightforward to grasp. A lot of plants have branches or stems that spread sidewise or horizontally, for which *horizontalis* is one apt name; another, equally obvious, is *radiatus*, radiating. Perhaps less clear are *patens* and *patulus*, both of which mean spreading.

Many plants are more laid back in appearance; they may be reclined, *reclinatus*, decumbent, *decumbens*, downward curving, *declinatus*, or, as we have already seen, *pendulus*. Flowers and other parts of the plant may be bent back or downward. Thus *recurvus* means recurved, while *reflexus* is reflexed.

Betula pendula

Tagetes erecta

Leucospermum reflexum

ascendens ascending
assurgens ascending
cernuus drooping, nodding
convolutus rolled up
declinatus downward curving
decumbens reclining, decumbent
erectus erect, upright
horizontalis horizontal
patens spreading
pendulus hanging, pendulous
prenans drooping
radiatus radiating
reclinatus reclined
rectus erect, upright
recurvus recurved
reflexus bent back, reflexed
revolutus rolled backward
scandens climbing, ascending
seclusus hidden
supinus supine, flat
suspendus suspended, hanging down
tortilis twisted
tortuosus meandering
verticalis vertical
vicinus neighboring

FRAGRANCE AND TASTE

Fragrance is one of the most under-used characteristics of plants that are grown in gardens. So often appearance takes precedence and forms that are perhaps not so attractive visually, but which have a beautiful scent, are overlooked. Those most in demand are likely to be those designated *fragrans*, fragrant, or *fragrantissimus*, very fragrant. Any plant with *suaveolens*, sweet-smelling, in its name is also probably worth having. *Odorus* or *odoratus* also means fragrant or sweet-smelling, as in one of the best loved of all plants, the sweet pea, *Lathyrus odoratus*.

However, there are also a lot to avoid. *Foetidus*, as one might expect, is foetid or stinking; *phu* has the same descriptive meaning. An equally obvious adjective is *pungens* or pungent. But things get worse. A plant with the epithet *hircinus* should be given a wide berth as it allegedly smells of goats! Not much better is *dysodea*, which means evil-smelling.

Not so many of our garden plants are used for food, or even medicine, these days, but a number still have names that reflect the times when every plant was potentially food or a medicinal herb. *Cibarius* and *edulis* both mean edible, and *esculentus* also means tasty. Plants named *dulcis* earn their keep as they taste sweet. However, beware of *emeticus*, as the plant acts as an emetic, and also of *inebrians*, which means inebriating or intoxicating. Plants called *nauseosus* are worth avoiding, for obvious reasons, although it may be their smell rather than their taste that is nauseating.

Picea pungens

Lathyrus odoratus

acetosellus	slightly acid
acris	acrid
altilis	nutritious
anosmus	without scent
aromaticus	aromatic
causticus	caustic
cibarius	edible
citrodorus	lemon-scented
dulcis	sweet
dysodea	evil-smelling
edulis	edible
emeticus	emetic
esculentus	tasty, edible
felosmus	foul-smelling
foetidus	stinking, foetid
fragrans	fragrant
fragrantissimus	very fragrant
graveolens	strongly fragrant
hedys	sweet, pleasant
hircinus	smelling of goats
inebrians	inebriating, intoxicating
inodorus	without smell
insipidus	insipid, with little taste
irritans	irritable, discomforting
nauseosus	nauseating
odoratus	fragrant
odorus	fragrant
olidus	stinking
phu	stinking
pungens	pungent
saccharinus	sweet, sugary
suaveolens	sweet-smelling
suavis	sweet
succulentus	succulent, juicy

FLOWERING TIME

Plants seem to make the most of any opportunities that may be of benefit to them. By natural selection they have found that flowering at certain times of the year, or even certain times of day, gives them the edge over their potential rivals in the survival game.

Two of the more obvious names that reflect flowering time refer to those plants that are annuals or biennials, *annuus* and *biennis*, while *deciduus* indicates that the plant has leaves that last for only one season (in other words, that it is deciduous). Winter can be a good time for plants to be around as there is little competition, although there is a lack of pollinators and inclement weather to cause problems. Any plant with *hyemalis*, *hybernus*, or *brumalis* in its name is worth considering to brighten up the garden at that time of year. With spring, things are getting under way; *praecox* indicates that the plant is early flowering, and *veris* (as in *Primula veris*, the cowslip) and *vernalis* both mean spring. *Majalis* specifies the month of flowering, May, as in *Convallaria majalis*, the lily-of-the-valley.

Summer is the height of the year and is represented in names (*aestivalis*, for example) only when other members of the genus flower early or late in the year. Plants that flower in the fall are well worth noting; *autumnalis* is the most frequently met specific name and one of the easiest to remember.

On a shorter time-span, many plants are represented by the time of day at which they flower, *hesperis*, evening-flowering, and *noctiflorus*, flowering at night-time, being but two.

Cyclamina vernalis

Bellis perennis

Colchicum autumnale

aequinoctialus	at the equinox
aestivalis	summer
annuus	annual
autumnalis	fall
biennis	biennial
brumalis	winter-flowering
deciduus	lasting only one season
epiteius	annual
hesperis	evening
hybernalis	winter
hybernus	winter
hyemalis	winter
majalis	May-flowering
meridianus	noon, midday
meridionalis	noon, midday
noctiflorus	night-flowering
oporinus	of fall or late summer
perennis	perennial
pomeridianus	afternoon
praecox	very early
praevernus	early season
serotinus	of late season
solstitialis	midsummer
tardus	late
trimestris	maturing in three months
velox	fast-growing
veris	spring
vernalis	spring
vespertinus	evening-flowering

HABITAT

Mountainous

Mountainous areas of the world have a very distinctive flora. Many of the plants that grow there have made the most of a difficult environment and have adapted so that they can fill a niche with little or no competition from other plants. These plants are not only of botanical importance but are also of great garden importance as they form the basis of rock gardening.

Many names refer simply to the fact that the plants are mountainous. The most obvious, perhaps, is *montanus*, as in *Clematis montana*. Another word that is not too difficult to decipher is *alpestris*, or alpine. Of similar meaning, but often also referring to the meadows that clothe the lower slopes, is *alpinus*. Some names are more specific to their habitat. *Saxatilis* refers to those that like to grow on rocks, while those called *rupicula* grow among rocks or on scree. Many plants come into flower all along the snow line and these may be named *nivalis*. The cold also plays its part in names; *glacialis* means glacial or of icy places, while *frigidus* and *algidus* both signify cold habitats.

Not all plants that like a mountainous type of situation actually grow in mountains. For example, many plants like the well-drained environment of dry stone walls, reminiscent of mountain rocks. *Muralis* indicates a plant that grows on walls and *cauticolus* one that is found on cliffs.

Many plants are confined to, or come mainly from, individual mountains and their name often reflects this. For example *Geranium himalayense* comes, as its name suggests, from the Himalayas.

Clematis montana

Aurinia saxatilis

algidus cold, mountainous
alpeste of mountains
alpicolus of high mountains
alpinus alpine, growing in
    mountain places
cacumenus of mountain tops
cauticolus of cliffs
convallaria growing in valleys
frigidus growing in cold habitats
glacialis of icy habitats
montanus of mountains
muralis growing on walls
nivalis growing near snow
oreophillus mountain-loving
oresbius growing on mountains
rupicula growing among rocks
ruprifragus growing in crevices or
    cracks
saxatilis growing on rocks
scopulorum growing on rock faces
    or cliffs

aetnensis from Mt Etna
baldensis from Mt Baldo
carpathicus from the Carpathian
    Mountains
emodensis from Mt Emodus
garganicus from Mt Gargano
himalayensis from the Himalayas
idaeus from Mt Ida
insubricus from Insubria, the
    Lapontine Alps
olympicus from Mt Olympus
omeiensis from Mt Omei
parnassicus from Mt Parnasssus
pyrenaicus from the Pyrenees

HABITAT
Woodland

Most gardens have an area of shade in them somewhere. This may be because of dominant trees or to the walls of the house or adjacent buildings. This has always been considered a problem for gardeners as most garden plants prefer the sun. However, by carefully selecting plants that grow in the shade in the wild, there is a much better chance of producing an attractive border. When choosing plants for these shady areas, look out for names that give some indication that they grow in woodland conditions.

Probably the two most common names are *nemorosus* (or *nemoralis)* and *sylvaticus*, both simply meaning of woods. The popular wood anemone, *Anemone nemorosa* is a good example of the first, while the equally popular *Geranium sylvaticum* reflects the second, although its range is somewhat extended to include wild or scrubby areas. Both will grow well in dappled shade reminiscent of a woodland and in a leafy soil that is commonly found on the woodland floor.

Sylvestris, as in the tall annual *Nicotiana sylvestris*, has a similar origin to *sylvatica* and also means growing in woods, or wild places. Both *sylvatica* and *sylvestris* can be spelled with an "*i*" as in *Codonopsis silvestris*. *Dumetorum* is another such word, covering scrubby, bushy woodland, in which, for example, *Helleborus dumetorum* is found.

Although plants with such names are primarily from woodland or shady situations, many of them can be grown in the open if the soil is kept moist enough by adding plenty of well-rotted organic material.

Anemone nemorosa

Myosotis sylvestris

dumetorum of thickets or bushes
hylaeus of woods
hylophilus of woods
latebrosus of shady or dark places
lochmius of thickets or coppices
lucorus of woods
nemoralis of woods
silvaticus of woods, of the wild
silvicola of woods
sylvestris of woods
virgultorum growing in thickets

HABITAT

Open Land

The majority of plants that are grown in our gardens come from parts of the world where they enjoy open conditions. They get the maximum amount of light and receive any rain that is available. Light is particularly important to these plants as if they are deprived of it, they rapidly become drawn and often unable to support themselves. There are plenty of names that indicate that plants come from this type of habitat and these should be used as a guide to the situation they will like in the garden.

Many of the descriptions reflect the kind of open habitat from which the plants come. Some, such as *ruralis*, refer simply to the countryside, while others are much more specific. *Pratensis* and *pastoralis* both refer to plants that grow in pastures or meadows; in other words, they will grow in a grassy situation and are good for naturalizing. *Campestre* is also used to describe plants that grow in the open fields and pastures.

On the other hand, *arvensis* refers to those that grow in plowed fields; in other words, they need to grow in bare earth – that is, in tended borders – and will usually die out if planted in grass. *Segetus* is even more specific as it refers to cornfields as in *Chrysanthemum segetum* (corn marigold).

Many open situations are dry and plants growing in them are very useful for gardens with light soils. Thus *aridus* means arid, while equally dry situations are conjured up by *dunensis*, sand dunes, and *sabulosus* and *siliceus* both mean growing on sand.

Anagallis arvensis

Cardamine pratensis

aridus dry habitats
arvensis of plowed fields
campestre open fields, pasture
dunensis of sand dunes
epigeios of dry places
ericetorum of heathland
paganus from the country
pastoralis in pastures
pratensis of meadows
pratericolus of meadows, grassy
places
rudis wild or rough areas
ruralis from the country
sabulosus growing on sand
segetalis segetus, of cornfields
siliceus growing on sand
solaris of sunny places
trivalis common, wayside
vialis wayside
xerophilus of dry places

HABITAT

Wetlands

Many plants have adapted themselves to grow in wet places, some simply in boggy or wet ground, while others thrive in the water itself. Most, of course, prefer fresh water, but there are a few that have managed to adapt to salt water conditions and these can be found along the coast and in salty estuaries. Not many gardens have salt water in them, but names that indicate this will certainly be suitable for coastal gardens where salty winds blow. Some names indicate that the plants prefer running water to pond life.

Some plants simply "grow in water," *aquaticus*, while others, which will be of interest to gardeners with ponds, grow "under water" – *demersus*, *immersus*, and *submersus* – or float, *fluitans*. The type of water is sometimes indicated; *fluminensis* indicates running water in general, while *fluvalis* is of rivers and streams, which amounts to the same thing. If the plants grow on the banks or beside these streams and rivers, then *riparius* and *rivalis* might be used. *Lacustris*, on the other hand, implies that the plant comes from lakes or ponds. Plants need not be standing directly in water, but may prefer boggy ground or marshes, in which case *uliginosus* and *palustris* may figure in their names. If the ground floods, then it may well be *inundatus*.

Maritime conditions are indicated by a number of names. *Marinus, maritimus*, and *oceanicus* reflect that the plants grow by the sea, while *litoralis* means on the shore. Slightly more specific, but of no direct bearing to most gardeners, is *insularis*, meaning that the plant comes from an island.

Caltha palustris

Rumex aquaticus

aquaticus	in water
aquatilis	underwater
demersus	submerged, underwater
elodes, helodes	of boggy ground, marshes
epihydrus	floating, of the water surface
fluitans	floating
fluminensis	in running water
fluvialis	in rivers or streams
immersus	immersed, underwater
insularis	growing on islands
inundatus	of places that flood
irrigatus	of wet or flooded places
lacustris	of lakes or ponds
limaeus	of stagnant water
limnophilus	of marshes
limosus	of muddy places
litoralis	of the sea shore
lutarius	of muddy places
marinus	marine, by or of the sea
maritimus	by the sea, seashore
mortuiflumis	dead or stagnant water
natans	floating underwater, swimming
nesophilus	growing on islands
oceanicus	near the sea
orarius	of the shoreline
palustris	of marshy ground
peninsularis	of a peninsular
pluvialis	of rainy places
porophilus	of soft stony ground
potamophilis	river-loving
riparius	of banks of rivers
rivalis	of brooksides, streamsides
submersus	submerged
thalassicus	marine, in the sea
thermalis	of warm springs
uliginosus	of marshes

RESEMBLING OTHER THINGS
Plants

All objects and concepts must have names if they are going to figure in our discussions and writings. One way is to give them unique names, but often it is easier to remember a name if it picks on some easily recognized feature. This feature may well be another commonly known object. In the case of plants, they have frequently been given names indicating that they resemble another, often better-known, plant.

In some cases it may be a generalization, such as *arboreus*, meaning tree-like, *bryoides*, moss-like, or *gramineus*, grass-like. Often the name refers to the foliage; for example, the buttercup, *Ranunculus gramineus*, has long slender leaves very similar to the blades of grass.

In other cases the plant is compared directly with another. *Jasminoides*, as in *Solanum jasminoides*, refers to jasmine, in this case to the white flowers. The leaves can also play an important part, as in *Ribes laurifolium*, where *laurifolium* literally means laurel leaves. As we have seen, the suffix *-folius* indicates a type of leaf; thus *quercifolius* refers to oak-like leaves while the name *salicifolius* describes a plant as having thin, narrow, willow-like foliage.

Even the roots of a plant can be compared; *napellus* describes a plant as being turnip-like or stump-rooted and the old name for *Rosa villosa* was *R. pomifera* because it has apple-shaped hips.

This type of plant name does not help the gardener in the cultivation of the plant, but the mnemonic value of such names does help the memory considerably.

Oxydendrum arboreum

Rosa primula

Campanula persicifolia

aesculifolius almond-like
amydalinus almond-like
arboreus tree-like
arundinaceus reed-like
betonicifolius betony-leaved
botryoides like a bunch of grapes
bryoides moss-like
caricius carex-like
citrodorus lemon-scented
dryophyllus oak-leaved
ferulaceus fennel-like
fraxineus ash-like
gramineus grass-like
hederaceus ivy-like
horminoides clary-like
iodes violet-like
jasminoides jasmine-like
laurifolius laurel-leaved
liliaceus liliaceous
napellus turnip-like
persicarius peach-like
pineus pine-like
pomaceus apple-like
primuloides like a primula
quercifolius with oak-like leaves
ramontioides like a ramonda
rosmarinifolius with leaves like
rosemary
salicifolius willow-leaved

RESEMBLING OTHER THINGS
Animals

If you let your mind run wild, it is possible to see resemblances in plants to things other than plants. Sometimes it will be the shape of part of the plant, such as the flower, that will remind you of an animal, or it may be some other feature, such as stripes or spots that triggers the association with a tiger or leopard.

You may have to think hard about some of the associations, but many will soon become apparent when pointed out. The curled flower spikes of the forget-me-not resemble a mouse's ears and give the plant its botanical name *Myosotis*. *Myosurus* refers to the mouse's tail, as in *Myosurus minimus*, the flower of which perfectly resembles the hind quarters of that rodent. (This plant is well-worth growing as it always intrigues children.) The cockerel has several associations with plants; *crista-galli* refers to its comb, while *crus-galli* to its sharp spur. The lion also has several parts represented in plant names, although often the plants come from countries where the creature is certainly not native. *Leonotis* is the lion's ear, *leonurus* its tail, and *leotodon* its tooth. Teeth are not always visible; those that give the dog-tooth violet, *Erythronium dens-canis*, its name are the plant's bulbs, found underground and perfectly shaped like a dog's canine.

Most of these names will not be of much help when you are selecting unknown plants, but if a plant contains the name *hystrix*, porcupine-like, beware: it is bound to be prickly. *Elephantum*, of elephants, is worth avoiding if you haven't got much space, as it is likely to be large when fully grown. However, *papilio* should be worth growing as it means butterfly-flowered.

Erythronium dens-canis

Panicum crus-gallii

apifer	bee-like
arcturus	bear's tail
buphthalmoides	ox-eyed
capreus	goat-like
cataris	of cats
colombius	dove-like
colubrinus	snake-like
crista-galli	cock's comb
crus-galli	cock's spur
dens-canis	dog-tooth
elephantipes	elephant foot
elephantum	of elephants
equinus	of horses
flos cuculi	cuckoo-flowered
formicarius	ant-like
hystrix	of porcupines
leonotis	lion's ear
leonurus	lion's tail
leotodon	lion's tooth
murinus	mouselike or mouse-gray
myosotis	mouse ear
myosurus	mouse tail
papilio	butterfly-flowered
pedicularis	of lice
pes-caprae	goat's foot
porcinus	of pigs
sauro	lizard-like
tigrinus	of the tiger
vaccinus	of cows
vermiculatus	of worms

PEOPLE
Men

A surprising number of plants are named after people, more than is probably realized as the names become disguised by their Latin endings. The specific name *okellyi* looks like a typical unpronounceable, unmemorable Latin name until you realize that it is named after one O'Kelly. Another name that is recognizable after a second's thought is *smithii*. (However, if the man happens to be Russian then things can take a more difficult turn, such as in *Iris zaprjagajewii*!)

Plants were, and still are, named after people for a variety of reasons. Perhaps the best is because they discovered the plant or were the first to introduce it into cultivation. Other less meritorious reasons are that the person who named the plant wanted to honor a patron, some notable person, or just a friend.

Men of the church have always been at the forefront of botanical discoveries. They have either discovered the plants themselves or been honored by plants collected in areas where they were missionaries. The most famous is l'Abbé Armand David, a missionary in China who collected innumerable plants. Many carry his name *davidii*, or *armandii*, his forename. Others went to foreign parts specifically to collect plants. Notable are George Forrest, represented by his surname, *forrestii*, and his forename, *georgii*, and Joseph Banks, with his famous *Rosa banksiae*. Some plantsmen had plants they bred named after them. *Clematis jackmanii*, for example, is named after the British nurseryman George Jackman.

Names of people used as specific names were once honored with a capital letter, but this is no longer acceptable practice.

Buddleja davidii

Phlox drummondii

armandii	l'Abbé Armand David
banksianus	Joseph Banks
banksii	Joseph Banks
Cunninghamia	James Cunningham
davidii	l'Abbé Armand David
douglasii	David Douglas
falconeri	Hugh Falconer
fargesii	Paul Guillaume Farges
farreri	Reginald Farrer
forrestii	George Forrest
georgii	George Forrest
Groenlandia	Johannes Groenland of Paris
halleri	Hans Hallier
hodgsonii	B.H. Hodgson
hookeri	Sir W.J. Hooker or Sir J.D. Hooker
hugonis	Father Hugo Scallon
jackmanii	George Jackman of Woking, England
jonesii	Jones
kelloggii	Albert Kellogg
menziesii	Archibald Menzies
okellyi	O'Kelly
robertianus	Robert
sancti-johannis	St. John
smithii	Smith
wardii	Frank Kingdom-Ward
williamsii	Williams
Wisteria	Caspar Wistar
wrightii	Robert Wright

PEOPLE

Women

Women are not so well represented in plant names as are men. Although the
majority that have gained immortality through their names have been the wives or
friends of the (male) collectors, there are a handful of women who collected and
have plants named after them in their own right. One preeminent botanist was
Julia Mlokosewitsch, who discovered the beautiful yellow *Paeonia mlokosewitschii*.
Primula juliae was also named after her and is a much easier name to remember!
This habit of naming plants after either forename or surname is shared with men.
The use of a common forename does little to distinguish after whom the plant was
named. Occasionally the name includes both forename and surname, as in the
genus *Juttadintera*, which is named in honour of Jutta Dinter, wife of a German
professor of botany. Wives are frequently celebrated in this way; thus Reginald
Farrer is remembered by the specific name *farreri* and his wife by *farrerae*.
In horticulture, as opposed to botany, women have played an equal part, but even
so only a few are remembered in plant names, although many have been
commemorated with cultivar names. That great gardener Ellen Willmott has been
well remembered, with several plants taking her name in the form of *willmottianus*
or *willmottiae*. As with many gardeners, she is also remembered by the name of
her garden, in this case Warley Place in Essex, Britain (*warleyensis*).
Of course, patronage has meant that plenty of plants have been named after
royalty and the rich and famous. Among such plant names are *victoria*, in honor of
Queen Victoria, and *imperatricis*, after the Empress Joséphine.

Primula juliae

Agave victoria-reginae

Artemisia	Queen of Caria
Barbarae	Ste Barbara
danfordiae	Mrs C.G. Danford
ecae	Mrs E.C. Aitchison
ettae	Etta Stainbank
farrerae	Mrs Farrer
florindae	Florinda N. Thompson
Helenium	Helen of Troy
hilairei	Sacrite Hilaire
hookerae	Lady Hooker
Humea	Lady Amelia Hume
imperatricis	Empress Joséphine
juliae	Julia Mlokosewitsch
julianae	Juliana Schneider
Juttadintera	Jutta Dinter
luciliae	Lucile Boissier
mlokosewitschii	Julia Mlokosewitsch
reginae-olgae	Queen Olga
robbiae	Mrs Robb
Tecophilaea	Tecophila Billotti
victoria	Queen Victoria
willmottianus	Ellen Willmott
willmottiae	Ellen Willmott

COMPASS POINTS

Plants tend not to understand political barriers but grow where it suits them. Some are restricted to very small areas, perhaps covering only a few square yards, while others are distributed over several continents. These widespread plants often bear names that show which part of the globe they cover.

The very far north, way up into the Arctic, is represented by *hyperboreus*, where very few plants are of interest to gardeners, except to alpine growers perhaps. Farther south, but still in the north, comes *borealis*. Plants with this specific name are bound to be hardy; *Phlox borealis*, for example, comes from Alaska, where it can survive temperatures as low as -49°F. *Betula borealis* is spread across the north of the American continent and is capable of surviving similar temperatures.

At the other extreme there is *australis* – south or southern. *Cordyline australis* comes from the southern hemisphere, but from New Zealand and not, as may be suspected from the name, from Australia. However, not all plants bearing this name come from as far south. In *Baptisia australis*, which comes from the eastern United States, the specific name refers to the fact that it grows at the southern extremity of the range of that particular genus.

One of the most frequently met names is *orientalis*, meaning eastern. East tends to mean simply to the east of Europe, anywhere east of the eastern Mediterranean – the Orient in other words. The word conjures up mystery and opulence, and many of the plants bearing this name are well worth growing – the brilliant *Papaver orientale*, for example.

australis southern
borealis northern
centralis central
hyperboreus far north
occidentalis western
orientalis eastern

Papaver orientale

Linnaea borealis

PLACES

Continents

Some plants show a very wide distribution, so wide that they cannot be pinned down to one country, or in many cases, even one continent, although they are likely to vary slightly from place to place. *Caltha palustris* is an example, as its distribution extends right round the northern hemisphere. There are many plants that are more restricted but are still endemic throughout a whole continent and this is often reflected in the naming of the plant. Not all plants that are named after continents are widespread, however; the name may well reflect simply that this is the species that comes from Asia as opposed to America, from where the rest of the genus may originate.

Because the areas involved are often large, such a name does not necessarily indicate the sorts of conditions the plant will require. Some Asiatic plants, for example, may come from subtropical areas, while others may grow in much colder areas. As a rule, most plants from Africa are tender, but even here there are plants that grow on the mountains that will be hardy in more temperate lands. On the whole the names are all very obvious and will be easily recognized by most gardeners. That *europeus* should refer to Europe, *asiaticus* to Asia, and *americanus* to America should come as no surprise. Africa is not quite so easy to identify in some of its forms. As well as *africanus*, it is also represented by either *afer* (usually northern Africa), as in *Ptilostemon afer*, or *aethiopicus*, as in the very beautiful calla lily, *Zantedeschia aethiopica*. The remaining continents of India and Australia are not difficult, but beware of *australis*, which refers to the south and not to Australia.

aethiopicus Africa
afer (northern) Africa
africanus Africa
americanus America
asiaticus Asia
australiensis Australia
europeus Europe
indicus India

Callistephus chinensis

Iris germanica

PLACES

Countries

Giving names to plants is not a particularly easy undertaking, but selecting the country of origin of a species is one of the easier solutions. Of course, plants are no respecters of national boundaries and although it may bear the name of one country, a plant is often found in neighboring states. The given name is usually either the country in which it was first found, or the one in which it is most frequently or typically located.

In most cases the name is easy to identify with the country. There are no prizes for being able to guess the origin of *italicus* or *germanicus*, nor yet *hollandicus* (although as well as meaning Holland and the Netherlands, it can also refer to northern New Guinea). Some names have been Latinized, but are still clearly intelligible; *novae-zelandiae*, for example, clearly refers to New Zealand. Some are a bit more obscure, but are still obvious after a moment's thought; *amicorum* is a direct translation of the Friendly Isles or Tonga, for example.

Take care, however, as it easy to make mistakes by assuming too much. The specific name *formosus* does not refer to the island of Formosa or Taiwan, it means beautiful; *formosanus* is the name meaning from Formosa, as indeed does *taiwanensis*. The suffixes *-anus* and *-ensis* are a good indication that the word is derived from a place name.

Another trap to watch out for is that some countries may be represented by different spellings of their name. Thus China may be seen as *chinensis* or *sinensis*, as in *Astilbe chinensis* and *Miscanthus sinensis*.

Asarum europaeum

Phytolacca americana

Trollius europaeus

afghanicaus	Afghanistan
amicorum	Friendly Isles, Tonga
arabicus	Arabia
austriacus	Austria
cashmerianus	Kashmir
chinensis	China
fennicus	Finland
gallicus	France
germanicus	Germany
graecus	Greece
hellenicus	Greece
helveticus	Switzerland
hispanicus	Spain
hollandicus	Holland, Netherlands
hungaricus	Hungary
islandicus	Iceland
italicus	Italy
koreanus	Korea
lusitanicus	Portugal
moldavicus	Moldavia
novae-zelandiae	New Zealand
persicus	Persia
scoticus	Scotland
sinensis	China
suecicus	Sweden
syriacus	Syria
thibetianus	Thibet
virginicus	Virgin Islands

PLACES

States and Regions

At a more local level, plants are often referred to by their region of origin. This may correspond to a state or county or just simply to a geographic area. The latter is particularly relevant if the area has a special geological distinction, and thus the plant comes uniquely from there. For example, if the name represents a range of mountains, such as the Pyrenées (*pyrenaeus*) or the Himalayas (*himalayense*), then there is a good chance that the plant is an alpine one, or at least that it is fairly hardy and will grow in temperate climates. It also probably means that it would appreciate a lean soil with a sharp drainage such as it would have in the mountains.

There are a great number of plant names that are taken from regional names, but many of the areas are relatively small and so produce only one or two names, for example Cornwall (*cornubiensis*). On the other hand, some larger regions or states – California (*californicus*), for example – have a very large plant population and may produce as many, if not more, names than many countries. Again, some hint may be given by the name of the region as to the conditions a plant may require. A plant from Cornwall will probably do well elsewhere in the British Isles, whereas one from California is likely to be on the tender side and may need winter protection.

Plant names are not always spelled as you might expect. Although *pensylvanicus* means coming from Pennsylvania, the double "n" was reduced to one when the name was first used and the missing letter was never restored.

Tradescantia virginiana

Eschscholtzia californica

adamantinus	Diamond Lake, Oregon
aleuticus	Aleutian
antipodus	Antipodes
californicus	California
cornubiensis	Cornwall
dalmaticus	Dalmatia
deodarus	Deodar State, India
dumnoniensis	Devon
emodi, emodensis	Mt Emodus, India
fresnoensis	Fresno County, California
garganicus	Mt Gargano, Italy
georgianus	Georgia, USA
georgicus	Georgia, previously USSR
himalayense	Himalayas
ibiricus	Iberia
illyricus	Illyria
ioensis	Iowa
insubricus	southern Switzerland
lazicus	Lazistan
niloticus	Nile valley
pensylvanicus	Pennsylvania
pyrenaeus	Pyrenées
rhaeticus	Rhaetium Alps
rhaponticus	Black Sea area
sudeticus	Sudentenland, Czechoslovakia
tauricus	Crimea
virginianus	Virginia
vitis-ideae	vine of Mount Ida, Greece

PLACES

Towns, Villages, and Gardens

Many towns and villages have given rise to plant names, although most have
produced only one or two plants of note and so are not frequently seen.
Needless to say, since we are frequently dealing with small towns and villages,
many of them are obscure, some possibly not even on a present-day map. Often
such little villages, perhaps no bigger than a hamlet, were out of the way and
may have been the only point of reference for miles around that a plant hunter
could use to pinpoint the plant that had just been discovered. Even the bigger
towns and cities are usually represented only by one or two plants.

In some cases the name of the town is an adaptation of the existing name; for
example, *stevenagensis* (Stevenage, where *Gentiana stevenagensis* was first bred).
However, in the case of older towns, such as York, Exeter, Paris, or Grenoble, the
old Roman name was pressed into use.

As well as towns and villages, many plants have been named after specific
gardens. This is mainly reflected in cultivar names, in which the vernacular form
of the garden's name is given; for example, *Pulmonaria officinalis* 'Sissinghurst
White', named after the famous gardens at Sissinghurst Castle in Kent, England.
Occasionally, however, the name of a garden occurs as a specific name, when it
will be Latinized. Miss Willmott's garden at Warley Place in Essex, England, has
led to the name *warleyensis*. *Kewensis* is named after the Royal Botanical Gardens
at Kew, which probably has more plants named after it than any other garden,
although most of these are hybrids that have occurred there rather than species.

Allium neapolitanum

Nigella damascena

Ageratum houstonianum

aleppicus	Aleppo, Syria
bonariensis	Buenos Aires
damascenus	Damascus, Syria
delphicus	Delphi, Greece
divionensis	Dijon, France
eboracensis	York, England
exoniensis	Exeter, England
farleyensis	Farley Hill Gardens, Barbados
genavensis	Geneva
gratianopolitanus	Grenoble, France
juanensis	Genoa
kewensis	Kew Gardens, London
leodensis	Liège, Belgium
limensis	Lima, Peru
lutetianus	Paris, France
massiliensis	Marseilles, France
matritenensis	Madrid, Spain
neapolitanus	Naples, Italy
neomontanus	Neuberg, Germany
novi-belgae	New York
pruhonicus	Pruhonice, Czechoslovakia
quitensis	Quito, Ecuador
sabatius	Savona, Italy
stevenagensis	Stevenage, Hertfordshire, England
tunbridgensis	Tunbridge Wells, Kent, England
vindobonensis	Vienna, Austria
warleyensis	Warley Place, Essex, England

FOREIGN NAMES

Although all botanical names are "foreign," there are some that have their origin in foreign words other than Latin and Greek. In many cases, as we have already seen, plant names derive from people associated with the plant for one reason or another and a large percentage of these are of foreign origin. But beyond proper names, there are a large number of species names that have been derived from the language local to where the plant is found. Often a given name will be a corruption or Latinization of the local name for the plant. Such names come from all over the world – wherever there are plants to be found, in fact. The origin of some words is relatively straightforward; for example, the genus *Grossularia* is named after the French word for gooseberry, *groseille*. Others have a slightly more amusing twist to them. Brooklime or brook speedwell, which grows in tangled masses along streams, has the delightful name *Veronica beccabunga*. The species name here is derived from the German *Bachbungen*, meaning stream-blocker. Another interesting species name is *antipyreticus*, which means against fire or protection from fire. This is the name given to a moss, *Fontinalis antipyretica*, which was used to pack around chimneys to avoid setting light to the roof.

Some words have been so thoroughly assimilated into the English language that they are now generally thought to be native words. The genus *Tulipa*, from which the common name tulip was taken, is derived from the Arabic word for turban. *Crocus* has a similar ancient history.

Digitalis purpurea

Veronica beccabunga

Ailanthus reaching heaven or sky
(Moluccan)
antipyretica against fire (Greek)
barometz lamb (Tartar)
beccabunga stream-blocker
(German)
bonduc hazelnut (Arabic)
camara arched (West Indies)
Ceterach fern (Arabic)
Cicerbita chickpea (Italian)
copallinus producing copal gum
(Mexican)
Crocus saffron (Semitic)
datura local name (Indian)
digitalis thimble (German)
Grossularia gooseberry (French)
landra radish (Italian)
Medicago a grass (Persian)
Nuphar lily (Persian)
Passiflora passion flower, name
given by South
American missionaries
Petunia tobacco (Brazilian)
Prunella for treating quinsy
(German)
Quisqualis Who? What? (from the
Malay)
Ravenala traveler's tree
(Madagascan)
sassafras Spanish name for
saxifrage
Tulipa turban (Turkish)
Urginea Algerian tribe
Yucca cassava (Carib)
zalil delphinium (Afghan)

CLASSICAL NAMES

Many plant names, especially generic names, have come down to us from ancient Rome and Greece, as well as from other early civilizations. As is to be expected of a system that relies predominantly on the Latin and Greek languages for its names, many of these names are derived from ancient usage. Plants have been studied from very early times, not only because they are a source of food, but also because of their medicinal properties and the very vital role they played in mythology, which in early times was an important part of everyday life.

In the first place there are many names that have simply been derived from their ancient equivalent. Thus *Anthyllis* comes from the Greek name for that plant, while *Mandragora* is the Greek name for the mandrake. Some names have been slightly altered from their original meaning but still have an obvious connection. *Allium*, which applies to all the onion genus, derives from the Latin for garlic, for example. Yet others have names that have been transferred from another plant, often long forgotten. Thus *Oenothera* comes from the Greek for ass-catcher, a task for which it is not at all suitable.

In the second place, many of the names derive from connection with the gods and other characters encountered in mythology. *Paeonia*, for example, is named after Paeon, a physician whom Pluto pleased with his cures, turned into a plant. *Achillea* was named after the Greek hero Achilles, who used it to heal wounds.

Achillea after Achilles

ajacis Ajax

Allium Latin for garlic

Andromeda Ethiopian princess rescued by Perseus

Anthyllis ancient Greek name

Cerealis, Ceres goddess of agriculture

Dianthus flower of Jove or Zeus

faba Latin for broad bean

Helenium Helen of Troy

Lolium Virgil's name for the plant

lychnitis lamp, as used by Pliny

Mandragora Greek name for mandrake

Morus Latin for mulberry

Narcissus youth in Greek mythology

Nicandra Nikander of Colophon

Nyssa one of the water nymphs

Oenothera ass-catcher, a name transferred from another Greek plant

Origanum name given by Theophrastus

Paeonia after the physician Paeon, who was changed into a flower

Paliurus Greek for Christ-thorn

Pandorea Pandora

phoenicius red purple, from a Phoenician dye

Polemonium after King Polemon of Pontus

Protea the sea god Proteus

Symphytum Greek name for comfrey

CULTIVAR NAMES

Cultivar names are the names given to particular varieties of a plant that are used in cultivation. They are usually given not so much as a botanical distinction between one plant and another but so that gardeners can make a distinction. For example, all cultivars of *Ranunculus ficaria* are botanically the same, but the different colors of flowers and leaves make it important that the gardener knows which one is being talked about and so each variety is given its own name. Cultivar names are given in any language other than Latin and are contained in single quotation marks. Before January 1959 cultivars could take Latin forms of the name and so, for example, color names such as *'Albus'*, *'Roseus'*, and so on were frequently used. Since that date only names in another language have been permitted

One of the most common sources of names for cultivars is names of people. Some are named after the person who raised the plant; others may be given to commemorate somebody. In some cases a famous name is used, perhaps to boost sales of the plant! Another source is the town, village, or (more commonly) the garden where the plant was raised or found. Some plant raisers use a theme for their names. Thus there is a whole series of 'London' pinks – *Dianthus* 'London Brocade,' *D.* 'London Lovely,' *D.* 'London Poppet,' and so on. Sometimes the plant might suggest the name by its appearance; *Astrantia major* 'Shaggy' is just that, shaggy. Sometimes, of course, it is simply the first name that came into the grower's head and has no relevance whatever to the plant.

Dianthus 'Bookham Fancy'

Dianthus 'Dad's Favourite'

Dianthus 'Ada Wood'
Dianthus 'Admiral Lord Anson'
Dianthus 'Alan Titchmarsh'
Dianthus 'Albus'
Dianthus 'Alfriston'
Dianthus 'Allspice'
Dianthus 'Ballerina'
Dianthus 'Beauty of Cambridge'
Dianthus 'Beauty of Healey'
Dianthus 'Belle of Bookham'
Dianthus 'Betty Buckle'
Dianthus 'Bookham Beau'
Dianthus 'Bookham Fancy'
Dianthus 'Bridesmaid'
Dianthus 'Buckfast Abbey'
Dianthus 'Crosswise'
Dianthus 'Dad's Choice'
Dianthus 'Dad's Favorite'
Dianthus 'Debi's Choice'
Dianthus 'Doris'
Dianthus 'London Brocade'

INDEX